JOHN MACK

MALAGASY TEXTILES

SHIRE ETHNOGRAPHY

2

Cover photograph
Merina woman weaving on a single-heddle loom.
From a painting by the Malagasy artist Rainimaharosoa, 1907.
(British Embassy, Antananarivo.)

British Library Cataloguing in Publication Data:
Mack, John.
Malagasy textiles.
— (Shire ethnography; 14).
1. Malagasy textiles.
I. Title.
746'0969'1.
ISBN 0-7478-0015-4.

Published by
SHIRE PUBLICATIONS LTD
Cromwell House, Church Street, Princes Risborough,
Aylesbury, Bucks HP17 9AJ, UK

Series Editor: Bryan Cranstone

ISBN 0 7478 0015 4

First published 1989

Printed in Great Britain by
C. I. Thomas & Sons (Haverfordwest) Ltd,
Press Buildings, Merlins Bridge, Haverfordwest, Dyfed SA61 1XF.

Contents

Acknowledgements

I would like to thank the Director and staff of the Musée d'Art et d'Archéologie of the Université de Madagascar, under whose auspices fieldwork was undertaken at various times between 1984 and 1987. I owe a particular debt to M. Ramilisonina, who accompanied me on three separate field trips and contributed greatly to my understanding of Malagasy ethnography in general. The work had the support of the Ministère de la Culture et de l'Art Révolutionnaires, Madagascar, and the British Museum Society.

List of illustrations

1
Introduction

The study of African textile traditions has always concentrated on the western side of the continent where production has been, and continues to be, especially prolific. There are to be found considerable variations in the materials used, in the technologies employed, the kinds of design applied to cloth and, indeed, in the status and gender of the weavers themselves. New innovations are constantly being documented.

By contrast, textile manufacture in eastern Africa has virtually died out. Indeed, it is only in historical contexts that it tends to be mentioned at all but even here none of the variety that characterises the textiles of West Africa has been recorded. The looms of which illustrations exist are of one general type and the cloth produced was characteristically a loose-woven cotton textile, sometimes with occasional warp stripes in dullish colours.

Only 400 km (250 miles) off the East African coast lies the large island of Madagascar. Yet here a quite different story is to be told. Hand-weaving in Madagascar is still an important domestic art and it survives despite the advent of printed cloth and industrialised methods. Furthermore, the variety both in the technologies employed and in the textiles produced is large. Some elements are comparable to historical traditions in neighbouring parts of the mainland whilst others are to be found nowhere at all on the neighbouring African continent. To such diversity at a technical level must be added the great profusion of uses to which cloth is put. At the most basic, as elsewhere, textiles serve as clothing, whether as dress for the living or as shrouds for the dead. They are also used to envelop sculpture, in particular that displayed at funerary sites or in funeral processions, and, on occasions, even to wrap up coffins. Beyond that, textiles have been tailored for use as mosquito nets, awnings, mattress covers and blankets, bags and, by some of Madagascar's small minority of Muslims, as prayer mats. In Madagascar textiles contribute substantially to the fabric of both life and death.

The Malagasy

Such distinctive, yet diversified, practice requires some preliminary explanation. The name for the island's peoples as a whole is Malagasy, the overall term used also for their language and adopted with an adjectival sense as a general description of aspects of their culture that are shared in common. As such it is used in the title of this book. Like all generalities, however, its use as a global term carries with it risks of imprecision. Thus, although the Malagasy language is mutually intelligible throughout the island, there are considerable dialectic differences to be taken into account, ranging from relatively minor variations in pronunciation to quite distinct local vocabularies. Equally, the island's population, numbering ten million, does not constitute a single people but is conventionally divided into eighteen distinct and named ethnic groups. Some of these are, to an extent, based in older historical alliances, but most are rather haphazardly defined, giving an often artificial impression of unity to groupings of people who may have little else in common other than their general region of residence or birth. Certainly, although the background of the Malagasy as a whole is extremely various, it would be a mistake to associate these ethnic groups with specific phases in the island's settlement. In general such ethnic names do not preserve a common identity but impose one.

The settlement of Madagascar
    Over the centuries the island has clearly been host to successive waves of settlement from a variety of sources. In more recent times the identity of such immigrants has largely been lost and it is now difficult to reconstruct in detail and with certainty the history of the voyaging that brought them to Madagascar's shores. There has been considerable discussion and research concerning the sequence of events. The main puzzle has to do with the Malagasy language, for Malagasy is an Austronesian and not an African tongue. The nearest comparable languages are spoken in Indonesia. In spite of the logic of geography, the structure and vocabulary of Malagasy are very closely related to languages spoken on the other side of the Indian Ocean. Bantu, and thus African, elements are few, whilst terms ultimately derived from Arabic are clustered in a number of areas, notably those that have to do with directions, weights and measures and time (months and days of the week).
    The first significant settlement of Madagascar is generally seen as having occurred some time in the middle of the first millennium AD. The composition of such initial groups of settlers is assumed to have included a substantial South-east Asian element, possibly the residue of a sea-borne migration which, over the generations, had gradually travelled round the northern seaboard of the Indian Ocean. A likely hypothesis suggests that

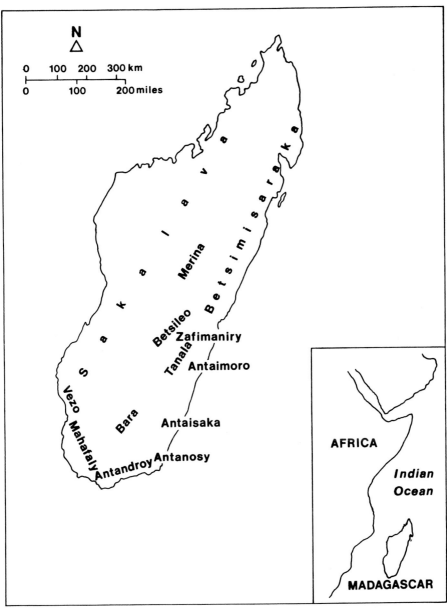

1. Map of Madagascar, showing the locations of peoples mentioned in the text.

intermingling with East Africans took place at a base (or bases) along the coast of the continent before the discovery and initial peopling of Madagascar.

Further settlement by both African and south-eastern and southern Asian groups has occurred in the intervening centuries and continued until recent times. Most of this must have been on a voluntary basis, though organised raiding by boat in the latter half of the eighteenth century, and into the nineteenth, also brought numbers of slaves from the African mainland and intervening islands to Madagascar. The raiders were Malagasy, some by that date the progeny of European pirate fathers and local mothers.

Arab interest in the island goes back to the beginning of the second millennium AD. The great expansion in long-distance trade links that brought the whole of the western Indian Ocean into contact with the Near East and beyond did not leave Madagascar untouched. The first stone-built mosque on the island was constructed along its north-western shores and dates from the thirteenth century. Islam itself, however, did not survive in Madagascar as it did amongst the Swahili communities established at such places as Lamu, Zanzibar and along the African coastline. This is not to say that reflections of ideas, practices and material culture associated with the Arab world cannot be detected in Madagascar. In practice, in the realms of astrology, divination and the healing arts, such influence is fundamental. However, all the island's present-day practising Muslims are descended from much more recent settlers or are affected by cultural influences originating in the neighbouring Comoro archipelago or the Indian subcontinent.

The European discovery of Madagascar occurred in 1500 with the arrival of Portuguese ships in the Mozambique Channel. Indeed, the disappearance of Islamic religious observance from the island is some times associated with competition between Arab communities and the Portuguese for control of trade in the area. In succeeding centuries the Portuguese were followed by other Europeans, principally of Dutch, French and British nationality. Of more recent European influences in Madagascar, two are especially important to our theme. These are the advent of sustained missionary activity during the nineteenth century and the establishment of French colonial rule in 1896. Of mission groups, the London Missionary Society in particular did not limit its interests in the island to evangelising work. Partly in response to requests from Madagascar itself, they brought with them

British artisans with a variety of skills to work and teach, especially in central Madagascar. The French, for their part, established a series of workshops in the twentieth century for the development of applied arts. These enterprises, too, are relevant to any consideration of contemporary Malagasy craft production.

Malagasy material culture

The range of these influences and the diversity evident in the backgrounds of those who have settled on the island are reflected in the field of material culture. At its simplest, the fact that people of Asian background played so prominent a role in the peopling of the island is demonstrated in such features as the complete lack of round (African) architectural structures on the island; all dwellings, including tombs, are rectangular. The African pump bellows is not used by Malagasy ironworkers; instead, piston bellows familiar from South-east Asia are everywhere standard blacksmithing equipment. At a more complicated level, however, the types of boat found in Madagascar include the outrigger canoe, the distinctive artefact of Pacific and Indian Ocean voyaging, the dugout canoe and versions of the Arab dhow. Amongst popular Malagasy games is that known in Africa as *mancala* (amongst other names) and in Madagascar by the Arabic-derived term *katra*; *fanorona*, a board game with Asian affiliations, is universal, and a local version of chess is also found. Similarly, musical instruments range from Arab flutes, through Asian styles of tube zither (*valiha*) and the cordophone employing a gourd resonator (*jejolava*), as used in many parts of East Africa, to the accordion.

Whilst parallels and affiliations can in this way be hunted down for many elements of Malagasy culture, this is a pursuit of uncertain value. Malagasy of African descent are not to be found playing *katra* on the seats of their dugout canoes to the strains of the *jejolava* any more than Austronesian Malagasy can be identified through a facility to play *fanorona* or the *valiha*. In practice, most of the features listed above are widely distributed and do not tell us with any clarity very much about the background of their users. Thus chess, *mancala* and *fanorona* are all likely to be familiar in the same region, quite possibly in the same villages and, although some are more associated with women and others with men, even played by the same people. Of the items mentioned so far, only boats provide a significant exception; yet even here the Vezo, for instance, who retain the use of the outrigger canoe, are in many ways the most divergent,

2. Raffia textile with the writing woven in as part of the process of production on the loom. The words are an invocation to God to bless the wearer and an evocation of the skill of the weaver. Betsimisaraka. Width 74 cm. (British Museum.)

not the most typical or the most Austronesian, of Malagasy.

With this in mind it is interesting to note that textile production is arguably the most diversified and the most regionally distinct of all the items in the material culture of Madagascar. Whilst, however, it is useful to point out some of the broader affiliations of particular techniques of cloth production, it is not the purpose here to use such evidence as a means of historical reconstruction. The intention is somewhat different: to provide a description of the variety of Malagasy textile production using the broader speculations about the island's cultural history as a backdrop to this diversity. This is done in the following sections, beginning with a discussion of raw materials, before moving to technological and design considerations. Yet in the end it is hard to avoid asking why textile traditions should appear to be the odd ones out in the material culture of Madagascar. Why should they be so diverse when many other types of artefact are, by comparison, fairly uniform in conception? This is, at least in part, a question of the use and significance of cloth, a topic which is raised in the concluding sections.

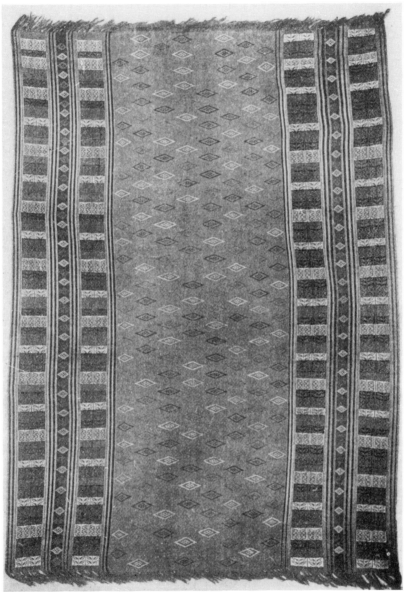

3. Silk textile with complex float-weave patterns in red, purple, green, blue, yellow, maroon and white. Merina. (Reprinted from *Notes on the Madagascar Collection*, The Philadelphia Museums, 1906.)

2
Raw materials

The multi-faceted history of the occupation of Madagascar is matched by the variety of the terrain the Malagasy came to occupy and exploit. There is no single type of environment or landscape that characterises the island. Indeed, the changes from area to area can be immediate and dramatic. Thus the eastern side of Madagascar receives high levels of rainfall and, though now to an extent denuded, it still retains large areas of tropical forest vegetation. By contrast, the central spine of the island is an area of high grassland, which is sparsely covered with trees, whilst in the south increasingly arid conditions produce regions of semi-desert. The natural raw materials available to the weaver, therefore, vary considerably across the island.

The commonest materials prepared for use in textile production are silk, cotton and raffia, which can be woven singly or in combination. The list of materials that weavers have exploited, however, is much more extensive, including bark or bast from various types of tree, banana fibre, hemp, aloe and, in recent times, wool.

Silk

Silk (*landy*) is arguably the most important fibre. It is the raw material for burial shrouds, especially in central Madagascar, and, according to nineteenth-century authors, is known in some contexts under the alternative name *Andriamanitra* (literally Fragrant Lord, that is, God). Yet there is considerable confusion over the origins of silk in Madagascar. There appear to be native varieties, usually identified as belonging to the species *Borocera madagascariensis*. Reports, however, indicate that in the 1820s Radama I, the king of the Merina in the centre of the island, was instrumental in the introduction of the species *Bombyx mori*, the Chinese silkworm, which is the most widely exploited species elsewhere. Other varieties were also tried out later in the nineteenth century.

There is a large number of terms in Malagasy to describe different qualities and types of silk. More than twelve are listed in one of the standard dictionaries. The basic distinction, however, is that between *landibe* and *landikely* (literally, the big and little silkworm). The former is the indigenous variety which feeds on various trees and bushes native to the island (*tapia* being the most

4. (Above) Caterpillars being developed in containers of leaves rather than on the tree. Photographed in Ambalavao, Betsileo. (Photograph: John Mack.)

5. (Right) Woman spinning cotton to prepare the thread for mounting on the loom. Antandroy. (Otto Peetz Collection, British Museum.)

common). *Landikely* is the local term for the imported versions and these feed on mulberry, which was itself brought to Madagascar from Mauritius for the purpose. A clever practice that obviates the necessity to cultivate the appropriate trees locally is found amongst some southern Betsileo. Here the caterpillars are acquired elsewhere and brought, together with the leaves, to the weaving centre. They are developed in a box in the rafters of a house and, when ready, the silk can be prepared.

The means of preparation vary. In the case of *landibe*, spinning is necessary and the discovery of spindle whorls in a number of archaeological contexts suggests that spinning (probably of silk, though cotton is also, for certain periods and regions, a strong possibility) is an old-established tradition. *Landikely* can be either spun or simply drawn out by hand. Amongst some weavers in central Madagascar spun silk is preferred for the warp and hand-drawn thread for the weft. To prepare the fibre by hand, the filament is simply pulled from the cocoon in a continuous length and rolled over a block of wood with the palm of the hand in order to twist it.

Of the resulting fibres, *landibe* is the more favoured by Malagasy though it yields a thicker brownish element that takes dyes less readily than *landikely*, which yields a smoother white fibre. The silkworm from which *landikely* is derived also reproduces over twice as quickly as native varieties. Cloth woven of *landibe* is, perhaps as a result, much the more expensive to buy even if it may be hardly more interesting in appearance than the rough thick sacking which it resembles. Silk production is especially associated with the Merina and their southern neighbours, the Betsileo.

Cotton
Cotton today has a much wider distribution in Madagascar than does silk. It was once considered to be a speciality of the south of the island and it is in southern Madagascar and amongst the southern groups of the Betsileo that cotton cloth is particularly common. From here it appears the production of cotton spread into central Madagascar. It is not, however, spun locally as much as it once was. Nowadays imported fibre and that retrieved by unravelling already woven textiles are the readiest sources of cotton fibre. Another common practice is to tie together strips torn from other cotton garments. These, when woven in with a warp of cotton, raffia or even lengths of plastic, give a thick blanket.

16

Raffia

Raffia is derived from the leaves of the raffia palm and is especially associated with the Betsimisaraka in eastern Madagascar. The environment here is especially favoured for the cultivation of the palm, as are a number of watercourses in parts of Sakalava country in the west of the island. Raffia, however, was also marketed widely, so that the exploitation of this raw material was much more widespread throughout the island than the raffia palm itself. Indeed, for non-Malagasy, raffia was, perhaps, the product most associated with the island. Colourful raffia smocks tailored and woven locally as clothing were acquired by nineteenth-century merchants, who sewed up the necks and armholes so they could be used as sacks for exporting other materials. (Betsimisaraka now do the reverse, acquiring plastic sacks and cutting necks and armholes so they can wear them for dirtier jobs in the ricefields.) Raffia came to be identified with Madagascar to the extent that the term in European languages is reputed to be derived from the Malagasy word, which can be spelt in one of three different ways: *rofia, raofia* or *rafia.*

The material used in weaving is easily produced from the inner membrane of the palm leaf. The outer surface is simply peeled back, giving a strip approximately 1 metre long. This is then split into separate threads by running an iron comb specially prepared for the job, or some other convenient object, along its length. Such combs have their teeth constructed at up to four different settings, allowing the width of the fibre to be altered. The weaver can thus control the fineness of the resulting textiles, some of which, despite their origins, have finished qualities comparable to cottons and silks.

Whatever the width, however, the length of each strip of fibre is never much more than a metre. Elsewhere in the world, in Zaire for example, this proves a limitation on the size of any resulting textile and separately woven cloths have to be sewn together to give larger dimensions. The Malagasy, however, generate the greater sizes needed by one of two methods. The first and most obvious is simply to tie lengths together neatly, cutting off any free ends so that the knot is often barely perceptible on the finished cloth. One author discusses the use of frames of various kinds to assist in keeping the threads from tangling as they are tied. Whilst this may happen, at least one of the frames described appears to be a warping frame which is otherwise used to assist in mounting the prepared fibre on the

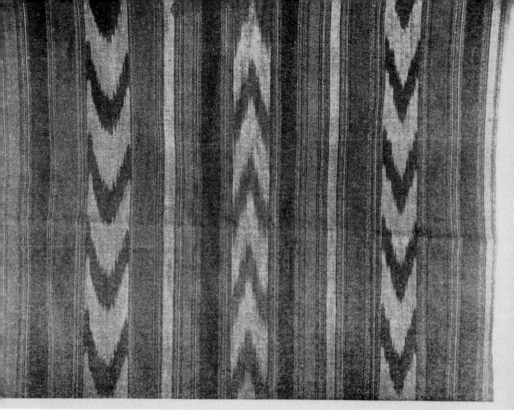

6. Textile in light brown, terracotta, black and natural colours. It is woven of a mixture of fibres: the warp is cotton and the weft raffia. The streaked bands running across the textile are examples of ikat dyeing. Such mixing of fibres in a single cloth is characteristic of some Merina weaving. (Reprinted from *Notes on the Madagascar Collection*, The Philadelphia Museums, 1906.)

loom. An alternative method developed by Merina weavers is to boil the raffia lengths in a solution of lye. This allows them to be twisted so as to provide the continuous thread. Either way, lengths of fibre are thereby produced in exactly the same manner as other elements familiar to the weaver.

Bark, bast and other fibres

Beaten barkcloth is produced in Madagascar as it is in Africa and in the Pacific. Its manufacture involves beating out bark with a wooden mallet in order to mesh together the fibres and form a felted fabric. Bark (*hafotra*) is also treated by various groups of Malagasy in such a way as to produce bast fibres which can subsequently be woven on a loom. It was once a widespread practice on the island, with evidence for its production amongst the Merina, Betsileo, Bara, Zafimaniry and Tanala. Nowadays it

7. Betsimisaraka men standing in front of a ceremonial site. They are wearing the raffia smocks which are traditional in the region. (Photograph: John Mack.)

8. Sections of bast fibre being rubbed together to twist the fibres and yield a continuous length suitable for weaving. Zafimaniry. (Photograph: Maurice Bloch.)

9. The commonest form of the Malagasy loom, here set up in a Betsileo house. As mounted, the heddle is suspended above the warp. (Photograph: John Mack.)

is effectively limited to the last two, who occupy adjacent areas on the fringes of the island's eastern forests.

The fibre is derived from a number of different trees but in each case it seems it is either a sapling or a thin branch that is used, not a mature trunk. Once the wood has been cut the outer bark is scraped away. This allows the inner surface to be removed in a single sheet, which can subsequently be split into smaller strips of a metre or more in length. These are then boiled in a mixture of water and wood ash, which assists in separating out the fibres. After being washed in fresh water and left to dry they are rolled and twisted on the thigh and knotted together to give a continuous hank.

The use of banana fibre as a raw material appears to have virtually died out and details of its production are scanty. The method involved beating the trunk of the banana tree until it began to disintegrate, to reduce its solidity and consistency. It could then be scraped to isolate the fibre, which was washed. The fibres were formed into a hank and finally boiled in a solution created with the remains of rice that had been burnt at the bottom of a cooking pot (and which otherwise is the basis of a popular Malagasy drink). This had the effect of rendering the fibre more supple.

Wool

The wool of both sheep and goats is used by contemporary weavers, especially in the south-west of Madagascar, where it is particularly associated with Mahafaly weavers. The introduction of such woollen textiles, however, is a recent innovation brought about by the French colonial authorities seeking to commercialise craft production. It has also been suggested that the need to diversify local exploitation of raw materials was related to the unexpected eradication of local silk cultivation by the inappropriate use of insecticides. The wool textiles that are produced are often made to be sold abroad as carpeting and incorporate motifs that are derived not from traditional textile design but rather from the three-dimensional funerary sculpture of the area. Similarly, the loom that is used is simply an upright frame imported for the purpose during the colonial period. It, too, bears no relation to the traditional looms of Madagascar which form the subject of our next chapter.

3
Weavers and looms

The conventional wisdom states that all weaving in Madagascar is the work of women (and thus a direct contradiction of the East African situation where, in historical times, weaving was an exclusively male occupation). The wisdom is almost entirely justified for it is only amongst the Antaisaka, in the south-east of the island, that Malagasy men weave, though even here there is nothing to prevent women from weaving.

Specialists and non-specialists

In the case of the Antaisaka, weaving is a specialist occupation. The extent to which this is also true of other groups of weavers in Madagascar can often be related to the purposes which cloth serves in any given locality. Amongst the Betsimisaraka, for example, any woman who shows the relevant aptitude might become a weaver. They may sell their products from time to time but they do not market cloth in a systematic way and sell only that which is surplus to their own family requirements. The Betsimisaraka use textiles as clothing, as covers for bedding and for other essentially domestic needs. Particular types of cloth are not reserved for ritual purposes to the exclusion of other uses. On the other hand, in central Madagascar, the home of the Merina and the Betsileo, special textiles are woven specifically to bury the dead in. Of these some may be used for the interment of those who have recently died. A number of years later, however, each body is recovered, re-shrouded and re-entombed; amongst the Merina, in particular, a further set of re-shrouding ceremonies also takes place. The number of shrouds used at the relevant season of the year is thus substantial. Clothing for the living, although nowadays mostly in European styles, is often completed by shawls worn by both men and women. These, too, are usually of local manufacture.

The demand, therefore, is sufficient to sustain weaving as a profession in central Madagascar and cloth is marketed extensively in the central highlands and beyond. Most of the island's best known weaving centres, Arivonimamo, Ambositra and Ambalavao for instance, are located in the region. However, such specialisation and such concentrations of weavers in particular areas also have some historical basis. As part of the experiments with craft production initiated by the Merina ruler Radama I, specific clans and villages were given responsibility for weaving, in which they developed particular expertise. Individual villages also acquired reputations as centres for the production of particular types of cloth or for specialising in the use of particular raw materials in their weaving. Such levels of specialisation have, to an extent, been preserved into modern times.

Whether or not weavers are specialists, most work alone: it is only amongst the Betsileo that it is common for more than one person to be involved in the weaving process. Here up to four women sometimes co-operate in the weaving of a single cloth.

The loom

Most weavers work in their own homes rather than in some weaving establishment. The character of domestic architecture varies considerably across the island, but many, perhaps the majority, of dwellings are of one storey with one room. In such cases weaving inevitably vies for space with other household activities. The construction of nearly all Malagasy looms, however, is such that they can be rolled up and stored to one side when not in use. The many misunderstandings about the extent to which weaving was, and continues to be, practised in Madagascar might be attributed to this circumstance more than to any other. Unless a weaver is working, casual observation will not reveal that weaving is a continuing local tradition. This, too, may be one of the sources of a long-standing confusion about the technological variety of the weaving apparatus found in Madagascar. One of the first and still most valuable accounts of non-European looms is that by Ling Roth (*Studies in Primitive Looms,* 1917). Included in this study is a report of the single type of loom that was seen to be characteristically Malagasy. Further, the loom was regarded as a prototype for other comparable devices once found throughout East Africa, which spread from there round the Sahara and into North Africa. Madagascar was suggested as the source of the diffusion of this loom type. There is reason to regard such looms as technologically related and to include in the list some Middle Eastern loom types. However, more detailed study shows that, across the range of features that are generally used in the classification of looms, the variations found in Madagascar are more substantial than was once realised.

The system of heddling

Beyond simpler descriptive features (such as the facts that all Malagasy looms are laid out horizontally and that continuous warps are everywhere employed), the aspect of their technology that is common to more or less all is the system of heddling used. At present the weaving found in Madagascar is dominated by mechanisms which use only single heddles (though this was not always so).

The single heddle, however, is arranged on the loom in a particular way. To understand this, some initial explanation of the general principles that lie behind the functioning of heddles is required. As the loom is set up, the longitudinal or warp elements are brought into tension and divided into two sets. Leashed to the lower of these is a series of ties which are looped on to a thin wooden bar; this is the hedddle rod, which is located above the loom itself. The upper set remains free. With the elements in this position, the weft may be passed through the gap between the two sets, called the shed, and beaten in to give the first crosswise thread in the structure of the textile. In order that it should be held in place, however, the disposition of the two sets of elements must be reversed and a countershed created for the second pick, or pass, of the weft.

The general function of the single heddle is to facilitate this operation. Lifting it up draws the set of elements underneath to the top, thereby creating the reversal required. The next weft may then be passed through and beaten in behind the first. Lowering the heddle rod returns the sets of elements once more to their original positions. By repeating these actions successively, a coherent woven textile emerges.

Single-heddle looms in Madagascar

Some accounts of Malagasy weaving suggest that the process of alternately lifting and lowering the heddle rod is the essential characteristic of Malagasy looms. It is certainly possible that some weaving on the island may proceed like this. The distinctive feature of Malagasy looms in general, however, is the fact that the single heddle is secured firmly in one position throughout the weaving process and is never moved. The familiar aim of reversing the relationship between the two sets of warp elements remains but this is achieved not by manipulating the heddle in the obvious way, but rather by moving a shed stick set into the warp system back and forth.

The loom works in the following manner. The weaver is seated behind the loom with the warp laid out in front of her. For the first pick of the weft, the heddle itself holds the shed open, separating the warp system into its two sets. The shuttle is passed

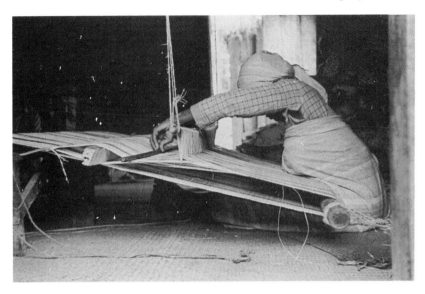

10. A sequence of four photographs to show the alternation of shed and countershed using the fixed single-heddle loom. (Above) Here the shed has been formed. Pressing down on the warp with the loose stick helps to separate out the two sets of warps at the point where they cross through each other. (Below) The weft is inserted and beaten in.

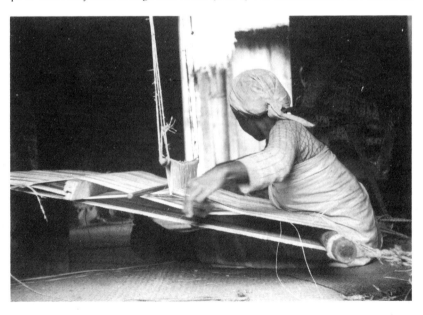

(Above) For the next pick of the weft, the shed stick is brought forward towards the weaver so it is directly behind the heddle. This allows the countershed to be created on the weaver's side of the heddle. (Below) The weft is then inserted and beaten in. All photographs are of a Betsimisaraka raffia loom. (Photographs: John Mack.)

through and the weft beaten in, using a weaving sword; this is a specially created smooth length of wood inserted across the breadth of the warp. This establishes the first crosswise thread in the structure of the cloth.

Beyond the heddle, as the weaver sits at her work, the position of the warp elements is reversed; that which is on the top in the section of warp immediately in front of the weaver is there underneath and vice versa. At the point where the reversal takes place, the crossover point, a large shed stick is located. The next step is to transfer this reversal from the far side of the heddle to the weaver's side where the cloth is being woven. Pulling the shed stick backwards until it is adjacent to the heddle brings the crossover point just beyond the heddle on the weaver's side. The wider the shed stick is, the larger the gap. It may, however, be further opened up to permit the passage of the next pick of the weft by inserting the weaving sword (which will be subsequently used to beat in the weft) and turning it on its side. The shuttle bearing the next thread of weft can now be passed through.

To return the warp elements to their original position for the third weft to be inserted, it is sufficient to remove the weaving sword and push the shed stick back and away from the heddle once again. Pressing down on the warps during these manoeuvres with a loose stick prevents the individual threads from tangling as they pass through each other. Although such a method of operation is capable of considerable technical refinement, this basic sequence of actions is characteristic of most Malagasy looms.

Methods of supporting the heddle. The most obvious and visible feature that distinguishes one version from another is the means by which the heddle is supported. There are several different ways in which this is done. Amongst the Betsimisaraka, the heddle rod is simply lashed to the rafters of the hut by long cords that can be adjusted as required until the warp achieves a suitable tension. A further set of poles arranged in the warp further along its length, and also lashed to the roof, adds additional support to the warp system and assists in keeping an even tension along its length; they otherwise serve no mechanical function.

In the centre of the island, on the other hand, it is more usual to rest or tie the heddle rod to two pegs driven into the ground on either side of the loom. A similar arrangement is associated with weavers in southern Madagascar. Here, however, the stands on which the heddle rod is placed are free-standing. Although this allows them to be moved along the length of the loom, the effect

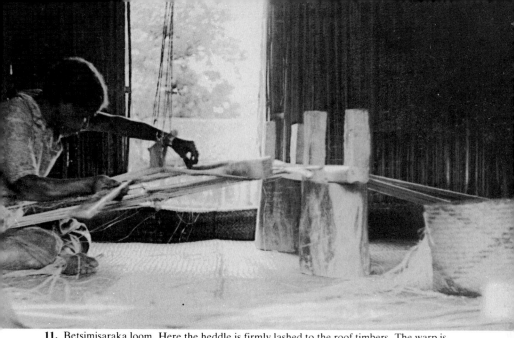

11. Betsimisaraka loom. Here the heddle is firmly lashed to the roof timbers. The warp is supported on stands which help to maintain tension. At the same time this device serves to increase the length of the warp that can be woven in cramped surroundings from what it would be if the loom were laid out horizontally. (Photograph: John Mack.)

12. Betsileo woman weaving a cotton loincloth. She works from the side, moving the heddle along on its mobile supports as required, a technique familiar amongst Antandroy and Mahafaly weavers. (Photograph: John Mack.)

remains the same as far as the heddling system is concerned: it stays unchanged throughout the weaving process, with the heddle permanently in one plane in relation to the warp, and the alternation of shed and countershed is effected solely through moving the shed stick. The use of mobile stands to support the heddle rod is particularly associated with the Mahafaly.

One other feature associated with the Mahafaly is that their textiles are woven on both planes of the warp simultaneously and not simply on one as elsewhere on the island. The mobility of the supports used to fix the position of the heddle rod is related to this characteristic. Thus, as the loom is set up, the warp is wound round two beams in a continuous length. This arranges the warp on two parallel planes. In most of Madagascar weaving proceeds only on the uppermost plane of the warp system. In these cases, as the textile is woven, the beams can be simply loosened off and unwoven sections of the warp system pulled round so they are accessible to the weaver seated behind one of the beams, that known as the cloth beam. This method has the advantage that neither the weaver, nor the heddle, needs to move in the course of weaving.

Amongst the Mahafaly, however, both planes of the warp are woven in together. Thus, as the woven section of the textile increases in size, it will be necessary to move the heddling system along the length of unwoven warp. This has the further implication that, from a position behind the cloth beam of the loom, the weaver would be unable to reach far enough to weave. For this reason the Mahafaly, unlike other weavers in Madagascar, work from the side, and not from the back, of the loom. The dimensions of the cloth produced in this case are obviously equal only to the distance between the two beams around which the warp is arranged and not twice that measurement, as is so when the two planes of the warp are treated separately. Although such characteristics are typical of Mahafaly weaving, the southern Betsileo use a similar system for weaving those kinds of cloth requiring smaller overall dimensions, as for instance in the case of a loincloth.

The backstrap loom. In order to weave adequately, it is important that the warp threads are held in tension and remain taut and untangled throughout the weaving process. As already indicated, the usual way in which this is achieved is to tie back the two beams round which the warp is wound, thereby stretching and tensioning it. This is the system used on virtually all African single-heddle looms. An alternative way of achieving

13. The backstrap loom as set up inside a Zafimaniry house. The wooden backrest is covered with a blanket. Pushing back against it serves to tension the loom in front of the weaver. (Photograph: Maurice Bloch.)

this result is to tie only one beam securely and to have the other, the cloth beam, immediately in front of the weaver, loose. Attached to either end of this beam, however, are cords which pass behind the weaver's back as she works, where they may be tied to some form of backrest. Leaning against this and pushing backwards enable the loom in front of the weaver to be drawn into tension. In Madagascar, it is only amongst the Zafimaniry, and perhaps amongst some of the neighbouring Tanala, that such a system is found, and the loom is used for weaving the bast cloth which is today unique to them. Backstrap looms are otherwise particularly associated with southern and south-eastern Asia: those illustrated in Ling Roth's influential survey, for instance, are from Indonesia, the Philippines, Melanesia and Micronesia.

Double-heddle looms

A final form of loom found in Madagascar takes the principles of the single-heddle loom on another stage. Here two heddles are used and not one. Each is attached to one or other of the two sets of warp elements. The heddles are composed simply of wood splints above and below the warp elements they control, with raffia cords threading them round the warp. A pulley system suspended above the loom connects the two heddles so that lowering one has the simultaneous effect of raising the other. Treadles beneath the loom are connected to each of the heddles so that their alternative raising and lowering (thus opening the shed or creating its reversal, the countershed) can be quickly effected simply by pressing down with the feet. This gives the loom type its alternative name, the treadle loom. In this case the movement of the shed stick is no longer essential to the weaving process; the heddles alone create the alternation in the warp system that permits the production of a coherent textile.

The nearest places to the island of Madagascar where similar types of loom are found are in parts of north-east Africa. They are also extensively used, however, by weavers at urban centres in the Middle and Near East and beyond. In Madagascar, however, their area of distribution has usually been said to be exclusively amongst the northern Betsimisaraka, although even

14. A double-heddle loom photographed in the Maroantsetra region. Betsimisaraka. (Reprinted from P. Heidmann, 'Les Industries de Tissage', *La Revue de Madagascar*, 17, 1938.)

15. Archive drawing of what is clearly a double-heddle loom used for weaving raffia cloth. This example was drawn in southern Betsimisaraka country in 1862. (Photograph: Gerald Berg.)

there their occurrence is scarcely documented. In such accounts as are available they have been said to be of ancient origin, which is also local opinion, or have been compared to European versions, suggesting a more recent derivation. They have been used alongside the single-heddle loom, also characteristic of much Betsimisaraka weaving, for the weaving of raffia cloth.

The earliest reference to the double-heddle loom has revealed that it dates back to the early nineteenth century. At that time, however, it was already said to be commonly used along the whole of the east coast. A drawing dating to the second half of the century shows a working example amongst the southern Betsimisaraka and confirms a wider area of use than today. Nowadays its use is restricted to a limited area around the Bay of Antongil in the northernmost parts of Betsimisaraka country. On the other hand, field investigations discovered that a number of Merina weavers could at least describe the main technical features of the loom and one woman in the area of Ambohimanga was found who had in recent times used it in preference to the single-heddle loom otherwise traditional in the vicinity. (She had stopped using it only when a pregnancy had gone wrong and the misfortune was associated by a diviner with the 'eccentric' equipment she had adopted in order to weave.)

The particular advantage of the double-heddle system is the speed and efficiency with which shed and countershed can be effected, which no doubt explains why it is amongst urban weavers producing cloth for a commercial market, rather than for their own domestic use, that it is found in the Near and Middle East. The essentially domestic nature of Betsimisaraka weaving goes some way to explaining the gradual disappearance of the loom type in the area. Betsimisaraka women also point out that, although it is quicker to weave using the double-heddle device, it takes longer to set the loom up, and once up it cannot so readily be dismantled to create space within the house for other activities. Thus special weaving installations protected from the constant heavy rainfall in the area are essential. For Betsimisaraka weavers the disadvantages of the more technically sophisticated device outweigh the advantages.

One other feature which distinguishes the double-heddle system is the facility with which, using supplementary double heddles, pattern may be introduced in the process of weaving. Most Betsimisaraka cloth, however, has only simple warp stripes if it is patterned at all. A further possible advantage of the double-heddle system has thus remained unexploited amongst those using the loom.

4
Decorative techniques

Decoration can be added to a textile either during the process of production or by applying it afterwards to the completed cloth. In the former case pattern can be introduced by using dyed yarn in the warp or weft, or by producing an effect in the course of weaving by deliberately varying the structure of the cloth. Decorative results may be achieved on finished textiles by dyeing, printing or embroidery, or by applying other material to the woven fabric. Dyeing almost always takes place before weaving and pattern is created through the process of weaving itself. It is, however, discussed here in order to group in one place technical details concerning the decoration of textiles. Appliqué is also a common traditional technique. Otherwise, the full range of methods of creating pattern has not been explored in Malagasy textiles. Printed cloth is mainly produced by industrialised means, whilst embroidery, like lacemaking, is a technique introduced during the nineteenth century by the missionaries and is concentrated in the central highlands, where mission influence has been the most sustained and consistent. It is largely reserved for items such as tablewear, which are marketed commercially.

Dyeing

Malagasy weaving exploits a full range of colours often brought together in individual textiles with striking effects. The sources of these dyes are various and the use made of vegetable materials in particular used to be extensive. Many of the plants exploited for these purposes remain unidentified botanically. However, amongst the commonest that are more fully documented are indigo, which gives blue; turmeric, saffron and the roots of the liana, all of which yield yellow; leaves boiled in a ferruginous earth, producing black; and the bark from the tree known as *nato*, which gives red. Oranges, greens and browns are similarly derived from plants native to the island. The process of dyeing involves immersing the cloth in a solution made of the appropriate substance together with either potash or a mixture of alum and tree resin, which acts as a mordant to make the colours fast. Since the 1820s chemically produced aniline dyes have increasingly been used, especially amongst weavers in the centre of the island.

The commonest decorative effect to be seen on Malagasy

textiles is warp striping. These are bands of different colour which run along the length of the textile and are laid out before weaving commences. The warp is prepared with bundles of yarn bound carefully and tightly together along their length, usually with raffia; this leaves one or more bands exposed. It is then dyed so that the exposed parts take the colour whilst those which are bound up resist it. The same procedures may be repeated, exposing other bands, to give a range of colours at the end of the process. When woven with a plain-coloured weft, these will appear as parallel coloured stripes.

An alternative practice is to bind together groups of yarn at intervals rather than to block out complete lengths of warp. After immersion in the dye, coloured patterns are produced which will work across, and not simply along, the textile when it is woven. Several colours of dye are generally used, with further effects being created by allowing parts of the textile already dyed in one colour to have an overlay in another colour. When properly controlled, such methods can yield complex imagery on the finished cloth. The technique is known as ikat and is perhaps most often associated with textile production in Indonesia, though it is found elsewhere in Asia. In Madagascar it is the speciality of the Sakalava and a number of spectacular large cloths woven in raffia have been collected. These show a range of geometric and figurative patterns. These remarkable textiles, usually identified with the Sakalava in general, are recorded as having been produced by weavers in only three villages. Though often taken to be so, they are in no way representative of Sakalava weaving as a whole, which is by comparison less complex. The production of these ikats had virtually ceased by the early 1970s, when the first serious attempt was made to document their production in detail.

It is rarer in Madagascar to find examples of weaving where particular effects are produced in the weft as well as the warp. There are, however, some important instances. The simplest are the occasional cloths with chequered patterns produced by incorporating bands of colour in both the weft and the warp. This is characteristic of some Betsimisaraka weaving, particularly on textiles intended for use as bedding. But much more elaborate effects can be created through the inclusion of supplementary floats in the structure of the textile, and some of the most dazzling of Malagasy textiles employ this method of creating design.

16. (Left) Dyeing bast fibre before mounting it on the loom for weaving. The pots directly in front of the woman contain the dye and the already dyed fibre hangs above to dry. Zafimaniry. (Photograph: Maurice Bloch.)

17. (Right) Detail of an ikat-dyed raffia textile showing two schematised human figures. The colours here are brown, black, orange, green and the natural colour of the raffia. Sakalava. (Field Museum, Chicago.)

Supplementary float patterns

The basic manner in which warp and weft intersect in a textile is in a relationship of one over and one under. The result is a cloth with a plain weave. Any other arrangement than this will cause one of the sets of elements to float over the other, an effect which will be visible on the surface of the cloth and which can be managed in such a way as to yield pattern on the finished textile.

There are a number of ways in which such float patterns can be created. In the case of Malagasy weaving, the most sophisticated techniques use one or more supplementary single heddles arranged in series across the breadth of the warp. Each of these is located beyond the main (single) heddle as the weaver is seated and each is leashed to a band of warps usually no more than about

150 mm wide. The warp between each of the supplementary single heddles may either be dyed, as in some of the older textiles, or plain white, as is more common nowadays. If the warp is dyed, the cloth when woven will have broad bands of weft float patterning separated by thinner coloured warp stripes. Such

18. A painting by a Malagasy artist which dates from 1907. It shows a supplementary single heddle suspended from high above the warp. Such a device continues to be used to produce bands of pattern along the length of the textile. Merina. (British Embassy, Antanarivo.)

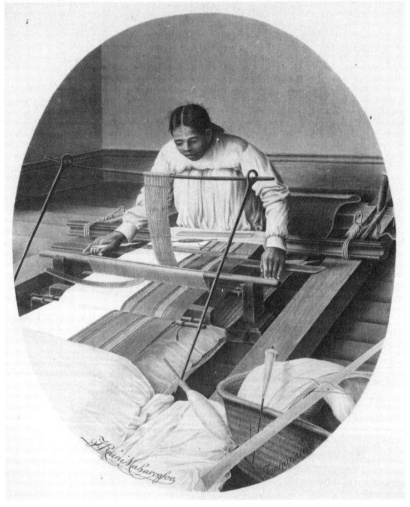

19. Detail of a silk textile showing supplementary float patterning. This is a particularly elaborate example but has been woven on a loom like the one illustrated in figure 18. The colours are red, pink, purple, several shades of blue, yellow, green and white. Merina. (British Museum.)

features are characteristic of some Merina silk fabrics dating to the second half of the nineteenth century and the early decades of the twentieth. The plain white cloth seems to be a twentieth-century preference.

The float patterns are all geometric in form, though they may be found in varying degrees of complexity. Each may be composed of up to fifty or so picks of the weft, though every second pass of the weft is usually facilitated by the principal single heddle and is beaten in behind a weft which floats, to give greater structural coherence to the textile. The method of creating the required patterns is laborious. Each individual design motif in the repertoire of the weaver needs to be picked out by hand, using the supplementary heddle to locate those warp threads that must be raised and those that will remain in position. From accumulated experience weavers have available to them an archive of different patterns. These are available as long sets of figures written out on sheafs of paper. Each figure in a row indicates which of the heddle leashes need to be manipulated for each successive pass of the weft in order to create particular effects.

The leashes are counted off from one side of the supplementary heddle and the weft will pass under those warps which are raised by the heddle and will float over those which are left.

The most dramatic cloths produced by these means have numerous bands of patterns in a wide range of colours, giving results which belie the relative simplicity of the technology. Some of the finest were reported in the nineteenth century to take five months to complete. Indeed, the London Missionary Society sent a weaver, Thomas Rowlands, to Madagascar as early as the 1820s to try to improve local production. A cotton spinner named Cummins followed. However, not only did they fail to produce any commercially viable product using local means, but they also failed to make any innovation in the technology, which, at its most impressive, was already capable of producing the elaborate float patterning. The technology in use today is little different from that which was current amongst Merina weavers when Rowlands died in 1826. Cummins returned home after only two years, without having made significant improvements.

Their efforts to place textile production on a commercial footing were almost certain to fail, for the purpose of the most prestigious weaving was to produce cloth not for mundane and marketable purposes but for sacred ones, as will be discussed in chapter 5. Only in the opening decades of the twentieth century was such cloth sold to any significant degree to outsiders. Indeed, by the mid 1920s it was reported that most was being made only for sale to Europeans. By then, however, the French colonial authorities had abolished the Merina monarchy, the last queen had died in exile, and much of the hierarchical and ritual context in which such cloth was used had been altered or dismantled. Nowadays such elaborate patterning is applied to shawls woven in white, and not in coloured, silk.

One final technique which employs float patterns is used by the Betsileo and is also seen on some Mahafaly and Antandroy cotton textiles manaufactured further to the south. As with Merina textiles, it is the weft which floats to create the patterning and it is either in white or coloured thread, whichever contrasts best with the bands of warp striping in the body of the textile. Such patterning, however, is found only at the edge of the textile and works across rather than along it, as in the case of Merina weaving. In this it reproduces designs otherwise applied to the finished cloth in beadwork, a technique also characteristic of some Betsileo textiles and used extensively in southern Madagascar.

20. Woven border in black, white and red on a Mahafaly cotton loincloth. Width 21 cm. (Musée d'Art et d'Archéologie, Madagascar.)

21. Woven border of an Antandroy cotton loincloth. The colours here are brown, black and white. Width 21.5 cm. (Musée d'Art et d'Archéologie, Madagascar.)

Appliqué

The beads used in appliqué are traditionally in white metal, either silver, as some have suggested, or, more usually today, lead. These are applied to the cloth by opening up the weave and isolating either a warp or a weft thread. The bead is then clipped round it. These can be arranged to form designs which are almost

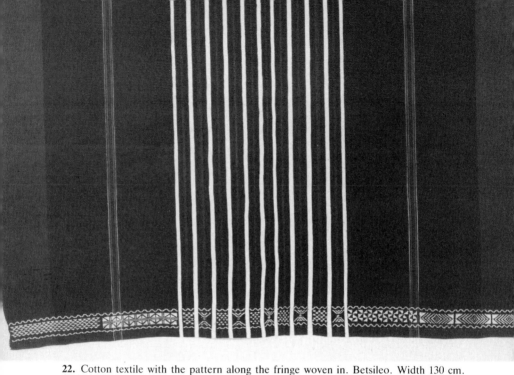

22. Cotton textile with the pattern along the fringe woven in. Betsileo. Width 130 cm. (British Museum.)

23. Cotton textile with metal beads set into the cloth to create a pattern similar to that woven in figure 22. Betsileo. Width 142 cm. (British Museum.)

24. Cotton loincloth with metal bead motifs. Antandroy. Width 21 cm. (British Museum.)

always geometric and similar to those discussed above. Again the techniques are most characteristic of Betsileo, Mahafaly and Antandroy textiles. Unlike the Betsileo, who are essentially rice cultivators, the economy and the culture of the other two groups are centred on their herds of zebu, the humped cattle of Madagascar. This distinction is also reflected in their textiles, for these often incorporate motifs showing zebu in addition to the purely geometric forms otherwise found.

As an alternative to metal beads, small coloured plastic ones are used. These, however, cannot be clipped on to the finished cloth and must be strung instead on to the weft in the course of weaving and be woven in with the warp.

5
The significance of textiles

For Malagasy the questions of design and colour of a textile are issues not merely of aesthetics. They are also associated with the broader context within which the cloth is to be used. A basic distinction is that between textiles which are used by the living and those reserved for wrapping the dead. The distinction is not an absolute one, for the dead may often be buried with their habitual clothing, whilst burial cloth is sometimes used for purposes other than for shrouds.

When a shroud is used other than in a funerary context it is not without a serious purpose. The shroud is still a significant textile and not to be used inappropriately. Malagasy feel a strong sense of irritation at the practice of some European residents and visitors of using locally produced burial cloth as bedspreads. In Madagascar, textiles which are intended for such essentially domestic uses are generally distinguished by being in different colours or incorporating different designs and patterns from those intended for sacred purposes. The main exceptions to this are the Sakalava ikats which might be employed for uses as various as mosquito nets, burial cloths and prayer mats.

The terminology of cloth

The overall term for cloth in Malagasy is *lamba*. The word is most readily associated with textiles that have not been tailored in any way. Thus, a shawl is a *lamba* but a shirt or smock is an *akanjo* or *akanjobe*, according to size. Separate terms also exist for skirts (*sadiaka*), loincloths (*salaka*) and so forth. There are, in addition, a range of qualifying terms used with the word *lamba* to differentiate aspects of pattern, use and materials.

Lamba, in the sense of a shawl, is a very widely used form of dress throughout the island, whether or not the other articles of clothing worn with it are of traditional manufacture. Thus a European-style suit or skirt may often be accompanied by a shawl worn round the shoulders and upper body. As such it is used by both men and women.

Colour terms are often associated with the word *lamba*. These do not, however, necessarily refer to the colours actually used, and not all cloth that incorporates the same colour would automatically be accorded the same name. The burial shrouds mentioned above are known generically as *lamb mena*, literally

25. Crowds gathered round a tomb at a *famadihana*. Virtually all wear the white shawl characteristically worn by participants. Merina. (Otto Peetz Collection, British Museum.)

red cloth; similarly a dialect term used to denote cloth used in mourning is *lamba maitso*, literally green cloth. In these cases, however, it is not necessarily the exclusive use of these colours that is indicated, for the textiles concerned may be composed of mixtures of colours, but rather their symbolic associations.

The significance of colour

In Madagascar the colour red is everywhere associated with the authority of ruling groups, whether it is mentioned in clan terminology (notably in Volamena, a Sakalava clan whose name literally means red money, that is gold) or characteristically incorporated in the material culture associated with royalty and with rulers. Thus, for instance, scarlet colours are familiar wear for important occasions throughout the island to distinguish those with authority. Amongst the Merina the sovereign's presence was evident from the red umbrella which shaded him or her on public occasions; similarly red cloth is uniformly attached by all Malagasy to their most powerful charms. The use of red suggests potent, ardent or forceful characteristics and, perhaps, even capriciousness.

Plainer textiles are, by contrast, frequently associated with those who are subject to authority. In Imerina, in particular, white was the colour of the *lamba* worn by commoners and slaves in the nineteenth century. Its use in other contexts is associated with cooling, protective, non-aggressive qualities.

In the context of burial cloth, the use of 'red' as a term has seemed to many contemporary observers to be a source of potential confusion. Although red may often figure in the cloth used for burial purposes, it is seen that it is rarely the exclusive colour used. Some sources have reported incidents where it has been the diviner or astrologer who has determined the colour and the pattern of stripes appropriate to the shrouds to be used on particular occasions. To that extent, it has been explained, red here means simply colourful and is to be contrasted with the white of the *lamba* commonly worn by the living.

However, any distinction of this kind is largely restricted to contemporary Merina. The Betsileo, by contrast, often wear coloured *lamba* rather than plain white, as do almost all other Malagasy. Furthermore, even in Imerina, the question has an important historical dimension. Thus, far from burial cloth having been multicoloured, a number of nineteenth-century sources suggest that many shrouds were then dominated by dark red tones (or at least had incorporated in the structure a uniform red weft), an association repeated in some of the dictionaries of the time, which frequently provide considerable cultural detail on such points.

However, the term *lamba mena* is in general use throughout Madagascar as the term for a burial shroud, whatever the local conventions might be about colour. What is implied is clearly the wider symbolic reference of red things: mystical power, vitality, authority. Red here refers to function, to features inherent in the context within which the shroud is used, rather than necessarily to colour. It is arguable that asserting these associations in the terminology used obviates the strict necessity always to include red in the composition of the cloth.

The use of the phrase *lamba maitso,* green cloth, as one of the terms for mourning cloth is again not necessarily to be taken literally. Mourning cloth may often be dark in colour, or become so through being left unwashed throughout the mourning period, but it need not necessarily be green.

Hierarchy of materials
Another significant element in the assessment of a textile is the material of which it is composed. Many of the early accounts make distinctions between more prestigious cloth, often described as silk, and materials worn by the poorer classes in

26. Sakalava woman wearing imported printed fabrics. (Reprinted from *La Coiffure*, September 1912.)

Malagasy society. Thus William Ellis, in his two-volume *History of Madagascar*, wrote: 'The ordinary dress of Malagasy is not only uniform, but simple. It consists generally of two, and at most three garments, which are chiefly of hemp or cotton, varied among the slaves and poorer classes, by a cloth inferior to either of these, and manufactured from the bark of the raffia, the banana, and some other trees; and among the rich, by the more soft and costly silk, or foreign casimere and broad-cloths' (1838, volume 1, page 277).

In practice such a hierarchy of materials was more characteristic of Imerina than elsewhere. For one thing, not every region had access to a range of materials. Amongst the Betsimisaraka and the Sakalava, for instance, raffia (the readily available material for cloth production) was surpassed in prestige only by imports: silk and cotton were not commonly available to local weavers. In Imerina, however, any limitation in the range of raw materials produced locally was overcome by the extensive trade in raw materials in which the Merina particularly specialised. Thus raffia was extensively exploited even though it is not a traditional product of the central highlands of Madagascar. The sources were both the west and the east coasts of the island and the main village for its production lay to the north-west of the capital. Particular Merina villages are identified in the nineteenth-century literature with the marketing of different raw materials.

Silk was, and is, undoubtedly the most prestigious material used and that woven from the native silk worm, the *landibe*, is more important than that derived from the imported *landikely*. Indeed, where the former tends to be the preferred material for *lamba mena*, the latter is more charactistically used for *lamba*. That does not mean that the nobility wore only silks. Amongst the royal Merina textiles were to be found a number of fine raffia *lamba*. The best documented is from the Sloane Collection in the British Museum, where it is said to have been the ordinary 'habit' of the queen. Silk was reserved for special occasions and raffia, such as this example, for everyday purposes. Nonetheless, the textile has a very fine texture and is woven with a range of coloured warp stripes comparable to those produced on the most complex of silks. To that extent, in addition to the materials used, qualities in the weaving were also esteemed.

Merina aristocratic fashions

Although the *lamba* is the characteristic Malagasy garment, amongst some sectors of Malagasy society there were considerable changes in style and influence through the nineteenth century, when the ethnographic documentation began to be accumulated in more details. Collating descriptions of the fashions adopted by, in particular, the Merina nobility across this period could give the impression of a kind of fancy dress party. Changes in styles of dress amongst the more influential elements in the Merina polity, however, had deeper political significance.

More traditional styles of attire for higher-ranking Merina can be gauged from the portrait of Rafaralahy, the governor of the Merina fort at Foule Point on the eastern seaboard of the island, which forms the frontispiece to Ellis's *History* (1838) and which was painted in 1822 (figure 27). Rafaralahy is shown wearing a long *lamba* with bands of warp striping in blue, white, green, red and yellow, with an edging that looks like a band of supplementary weft patterning across the fringes of the textile. The

27. (Left) The Merina Governor of the fort at Foule Point wearing an elaborate coloured textile with bands of pattern along its length. The painting dates from 1822. (Reprinted from William Ellis, *History of Madagascar*, volume 1, 1838.)

28. (Right) Merina aristocrat wearing the silk textile appropriate to his rank. (Reprinted from William Ellis, *History of Madagascar*, volume 1, 1838.)

sheen on the broadest band incorporated in its lengthwise construction suggests that a bolt of imported blue velvet has been included with what is otherwise, presumably, a native-woven silk textile. The hat he wears is also of coloured cloth with, attached to it, silver ornaments whose form recalls crocodile teeth, a powerful charm in Madagascar.

Imported coloured velvet became a popular part of aristocratic dress and the arrangement of the colours themselves was associated with particular grades in the Merina hierarchy. For example, blue was also a royal colour. It seems likely that the locally woven silk textiles with complex float patterns already referred to were similarly used to distinguish grades within the aristocracy, the design as well as the stripes of colour encoding political rank. Such textiles, according to some reports, appear to have been used both as garments for specific occasions and as shrouds. It was this unique combination of functions that made

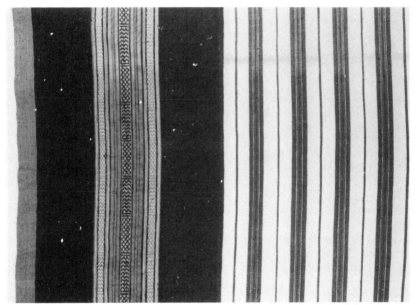

29. Detail of a silk textile in red, black, blue, yellow, green and purple. It incorporates bands of float-weave pattern. (British Museum.)

the attempt by mission artisans in the nineteenth century to market them systematically quite inappropriate.

Radama I, the Merina king who ruled between 1810 and 1828, was, by contrast with Rafaralahy, portrayed in the offical portrait by Coppalle in Napoleonic uniform, reflecting his admiration for the exploits and conquests of his European contemporary (figure 30). Increasingly, such European styles of dress began to acquire a certain prestige amongst the nobility in the capital. Similarly, the Merina army was attired in uniform derived from European styles of the time. The collections still preserved in the royal palace at Antananarivo include a range of royal and courtly attire that gives an impression of the development of nineteenth-century European fashions comparable to that which might be formed in a survey of the costumes of an institution such as the Victoria and Albert Museum.

As the relationship of the Merina monarchy and their European contacts waxed and waned over the nineteenth century, so, too, did fashions of dress. A particularly low point in relations was reached in the decade before the middle of the century. During this period the Merina queen Ranavalona I

30. (Left) Radama I (1792-1828) from the painting by Coppalle. (Queen's Palace, Antananarivo.)

31. (Below) Details of a patterned silk textile in red, mauve, shades of blue, green, yellow and white. Merina. (British Museum.)

32. Contemporary white silk cloth, the pattern no longer emphasised in colour but nonetheless still visible on the textile. (British Museum.)

reversed the policy of her imediate predecessor and expelled both traders and missionaries from the island. The attitude during these times was distinctly anti-Christian, with a strong prererence for the traditions that preceded the advent of sustained European influence amongst the Merina. Thus, on a return visit, William Ellis found only the queen herself attired more or less as before, while the members of the royal court were now dressed entirely in Arab costume. The prince, for example, wore a coloured silk robe and a green silk turban with a gold crescent in the centre.

Nowadays such exploitation of a large range of colours and sumptuous materials has largely been abandoned by the Merina. One indication of this is that the locally woven silks, which the mission artisans failed to market successfully in the early nineteenth century, were already being sold to outsiders shortly after the beginning of the twentieth century. In the intervening years the imposition of colonial rule had led to the dismantling of much that was overt in the hierarchical structure of the Merina kingdom. Most such textiles in Imerina are now white. They do, however, often incorporate, also in white, the complex float-weave patterns formerly picked out by the use of coloured thread. They have thus become less ostentatious but remain prestigious textiles to own and wear. One weaver has successfully copied a series of patterns from the decoration preserved on the walls of the royal palace. She retained the *lamba* for herself, but only for wearing to church, important ritual occasions and, ultimately, for her own burial.

Second burials

Madagascar is conventionally identified in anthropological writing as one of the homes of second burial. This is the practice of exhuming the dead, often many years after death and the initial interment, to complete the burial procedures. The remains are re-wrapped in a fresh shroud or shrouds and replaced in the tomb or coffin. It is an aspect of funerary procedures otherwise particularly associated with Indonesia.

Such ceremonies are not general throughout the whole of Madagascar. It is in particular the peoples of the central highlands and the northern Betsimisaraka who traditionally retrieve corpses for subsequent reburial. The Merina, for their part, in addition to recovering individual corpses, hold other festivals at which numbers of older remains will be re-shrouded, sometimes taking advantage of a second burial that is already to take place and sometimes specially arranged. Such events are called *famadihana*. The fact that burial rites are phased in this

33. Mourners gathered before a shrouded corpse. Merina. (Otto Peetz Collection, British Museum.)

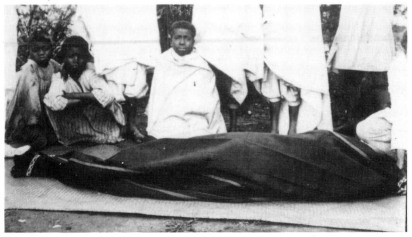

34. Women sitting with the shrouded remains of the occupants of a tomb (here covered by printed cloth) which have been moved to a new burial site. The accordionist plays for the ancestors as much as for the participants. Betsimisaraka. (Photograph: John Mack.)

35. Just as bodies are shrouded, so also the Malagasy wrap in cloth the memorial stones set up to those who have been lost at sea or have died far from home and cannot be buried in the family tomb. This is the ceremony at which such stones are installed. Betsimisaraka. (Photograph: John Mack.)

manner goes some way to explaining why the production and use of shrouds should be so extensive.

Second burials, or *famadihana*, are also seasonal events. They must take place in the dry season, that is roughly during the months of July to October. This is appropriate because the broader concept behind the phasing of burial rites as a whole is the notion that to be capable of passing blessings to the living (a crucial function of 'the ancestors') the dead must have become dry. The interval between first and second burial is at least partly to ensure that flesh and bone have become separated, that the remains are as nearly as possible skeletal. The assertion and celebration of this in festivals which take place only during the dry season renders the manufacture, and more especially the marketing, of the relevant cloth a seasonal activity.

The decision to begin arranging an event such as a second burial depends on many factors, some more pragmatic than others. One of the main reasons often given for the timing, however, is that someone closely related to the deceased has been visited in dreams by the dead. Their deceased relative has complained that he or she is suffering from the cold on account of the deteriorating state of the original shroud. To that extent the shroud is conceived as clothing for the dead. The fact that the thicker *landibe* is the preferred material reflects this concern with the most resistant and most durable of the textiles.

Cloth and spirit possession

Finally we should note that for living people to don burial cloth is a presumptuous act undertaken only by those with genuine power, whether political or mystical. The example of the Merina aristocracy who reserved the right to wear mantles that might also be used for burial purposes has already been mentioned. Similar practices exist elsewhere. The leaders of powerful Antaimoro clans, for instance, wrap themselves in burial shrouds for their investitures and subsequently wear such cloth at important ritual events such as circumcision. Nowadays Betsileo burial cloth is imported for the purpose.

The association of shrouds with spirit possession cults is particularly notable. Amongst the Sakalava second burial is not practised. Even the once and for all burial of royalty which takes place is not the spectacular event that might be expected, and royal tombs, by contrast with those of some commoners, are unremarkable. The reason is that in a cultural sense royalty never die. Instead, at the physical death the spirit possesses a

36. An Antanosy girl with hair untressed and wearing a Swahili style of hat to indicate the African identity of the spirit by whom she is possessed. (Photograph: Jeremy Marre.)

commoner. The person thus possessed goes to live in the royal compound along with the spirit mediums of all the other royal dead. At the death of the medium, the royal spirit inhabits another subject. In this way the whole royal dynasty remains extant through the practice of possession. Amongst the many functions of a medium is that of healing, a power used in the possessed state. Such powers ultimately derive from royalty, and spirit mediums emphasise this authority by wearing a shroud. This act not only establishes the identity of the possessed with the royal spirit but also asserts the potency of the powers acquired by the medium during possession.

Elsewhere in Madagascar persons possessed may be capable of acting successively as mediums for numerous spirits in the course of a single seance. Such spirits are frequently of exotic origin and the most powerful are generally held to be those of the Sakalava. Even non-Sakalava from quite distant parts of the island may be possessed by Sakalava royalty. Each of the possessing spirits is identified separately and again this is done principally through the use of cloth (though Europeans, for example, may sometimes be identified by some other item such as a cigarette or sunglasses). Particular types of cloth, and the imitation of particular ways of wearing it, may indicate possession by African or Arab spirits or by those of other ethnic groups within Madagascar.

6
Museums

United Kingdom

Birmingham Museum and Art Gallery, Chamberlain Square, Birmingham B3 3DH. Telephone: 021-235 2834.

Cambridge University Museum of Archaeology and Anthropology, Downing Street, Cambridge CB2 3DZ. Telephone: 0223 337733 or 333516.

Horniman Museum, London Road, Forest Hill, London SE23 3PQ. Teoephone: 01-699 1872.

Museum of Mankind (The Ethnography Department of the British Museum), 6 Burlington Gardens, London W1X 2EX. Telephone: 01-437 2224 or 2228.

Pitt Rivers Museum, South Parks Road, Oxford OX1 3PP. Telephone: 0865 270927.

Royal Museum of Scotland, Chambers Street, Edinburgh EH1 1JF. Telephone: 031-225 7534.

France

Musée de l'Homme, Palais de Chaillot, Place du Trocadéro, 75016 Paris.

Madagascar

Musée d'Art et d'Archéologie, 18 Rue de Dr Villette, Isoraka, Antananarivo.

United States

American Museum of Natural History, 79th Street and Central Park West, New York, NY 10024.

Field Museum of Natural History, Roosevelt Road at Lake Shore Drive, Chicago, Illinois 60605.

National Museum of African Art, Smithsonian Institution, 1000 Jefferson Drive, SW, Washington DC 20560.

National Museum of Natural History, 10th Street and Constitution Avenue NW, Washington DC 20560.

Peabody Museum of Archaeology and Ethnology, 11 Divinity Avenue, Cambridge, Massachusetts 02138.

The Textile Museum, 2320 South Street, NW, Washington DC 20008.

University Museum, University of Pennsylvania, 33rd and Spruce Streets, Philadelphia, Pennsylvania 19104.

7
Further reading

Dubois, H. M. *Monographie des Betsileo*. Institut d'Ethnologie, Paris, 1938.

Edmonds, W. J. 'Bye-gone Ornamentation and Dress amongst the Hova Malagasy', *Antananarivo Annual*, XXII (1896), 469-77.

Heidmann, Pierre. 'Les Industries de Tissage', *La Revue de Madagascar*, 17 (1937), 93-120.

Heurtebize, G., and Rakotoarisoa, J-A. 'Notes sur la Confection des Tissues de Type Ikat à Madagascar', *Archipel*, VII (1974), 67-81.

Mack, John. *Madagascar, Island of the Ancestors*. British Museum Publications, London, 1986.

Mack, John. 'Women, Weaving, and the Ancestors', *Indonesia Circle*, 42 (March 1987), 76-91.

Picton, John, and Mack, John. *African Textiles*. British Museum Publications, London, second edition 1989.

Vernier, J. 'Etude sur la Fabrication des *Lambamena*', *Journal de la Societé des Africanistes*, XXIV (1964), 7-34.

Index

Page numbers in italic refer to illustrations.